About Pets **editorial team**

Goldfish

Everything you need to know about keeping, caring for and breeding goldfish

Contents

Foreword 4

In general 6
    Origins 6
    Fish or miniature? 7
    Appearance 7
    Feeding in the wild 7
    A closer look at the goldfish: Ichthyology 8
    Movement 8
    Breathing 8
    Blood circulation 8
    Digestion 9
    The swim bladder 9
    Nervous system 11
    Hearing 11

Feeding your goldfish 12
    Water layers and feeding 12
    How much food? 12
    Types of food 12
    Live food 13
    Frozen food 13
    Dry food 13

A home for your goldfish 14
    The pros and cons of a fishbowl 14
    Water surface 14
    Furniture 15
    Housekeeping 15
    The pros and cons of an aquarium 15
    A place for an aquarium 15
    Light 16
    Aquarium types 17
    Dimensions 17

Things you need for an aquarium 18
    Cover panel 18
    Light hoods 18
    Heating elements 19
    Thermometers 20
    Filters 21
    Air pump 21
    Fishnet 22
    Aquarium cleaners 22
    Cleaning the floor 22
    Caring for an aquarium 23
    Fish and stress 23
    The aquarium water 23
    Water contamination 24

Plants in an aquarium 28
    Why plants are so important 28
    Plastic plants or living plants? 28
    Living plants 29
    Plant lighting 30
    Location and underfloor 30

Goldfish

contents

Plants for the aquarium	30
Winter Sprite (*Ceratopteris thalicroides*)	30
Cryptocoryne	31
Java fern (*Microsorium pteropus*)	31
Aponogeton varieties	32
Sword plants (*Echinodorous*)	33
Vallis varieties	34
Myriophyllum (milfoil or foxtail) varieties	34
Hygrophila varieties	35

Setting up an aquarium — 36
Checking the tank	36
Gravel	36
Nutrient soil	36
Rocks	38
Filling your aquarium	38
Fitting the heating element and thermostat	39
Planting	39
After planting	39
Populating your aquarium	40
Buying goldfish	40
Some important tips	41
The first week	41

The goldfish and its varieties — 44
The Common Goldfish	44
The Comet Fish	45
The Shubunkin	45
The Fantail	46
The Ryukin	46
The Japanese Goldfish or Wakin	47
The Telescope fish (Demekin)	48
The Celestial	49
The Moor	49
The Water Bubble-Eye	49
The Oranda	51
The Lionhead	51

Breeding goldfish — 52
Gender differences	52
Preparation	52
Mating behavior and spawning	53
Development of the young	54
Bringing up the young	55

Fish ailments — 56
Medications	56
Swim bladder paralysis	56
White spot or "Ich"	57
The Freshwater Louse (*Argulus foliaceus*)	57
Anchorworm	59
Tumors	59
Velvet	59
Fungal infections	59
Disinfection	59

Sources of information on the Internet — 62

Profiles of goldfish — 64

Foreword

Goldfish are among the most popular pets in this country, but sadly they're also one of the most neglected.

Once the early enthusiasm has waned, they get scant attention, are fed a little dried food now and again and are forgotten until the next time, or until the day a poor fish drifts belly-up on the surface. The reason behind this misery is that most people don't know exactly how goldfish should be kept and cared for, despite the fact that goldfish can make fascinating pets and, with proper care, can live for many years.

Instead of buying a fish and fishbowl on impulse, we recommend you first find out what you need to know to really enjoy this fascinating hobby. Once you know what and why, you will discover that there are many aspects to keeping and breeding goldfish, and you will automatically derive more pleasure from it. Furthermore, your goldfish will be better for it and not give up the ghost after just a few weeks. This small book will put you on the right track. It will show you that a hobby begun well can be full of happy moments.

Tanya M. Henning-Vriends was born in the Hague, the Netherlands, but moved as a child with her parents to the United States. After high school, she studied art history, biology, and business studies at the University of Cincinnati, Ohio. After earning her degree, she worked for a well-known publisher in New York. Together with her father, the renowned biologist and aviculturalist Professor Dr. Thijs Vriends, she has published various biology and animal books.

The *About Pets* editorial team

ibooks

All rights reserved, including the right to reproduce this book or portions thereof in any form whatsoever. Distributed by Simon & Schuster, Inc. 1230 Avenue of the Americas, New York, NY 10020

ibooks, inc.
24 West 25th Street
New York, NY 10010

The ibooks World Wide Web Site Address is:
http://www.ibooks.net

ISBN 0-7434-4528-7
First ibooks, inc. printing
November 2002
10 9 8 7 6 5 4 3 2 1

Senior Consultant Lisa K. Allen, DVM
Cover photograph
copyright © 2002 PhotoDisc, Inc.
Cover design by j. vita

As the purchaser of this book, you are entitled to access a free electronic book version of the title for use with Windows, Macintosh and Palm computers and PDAs. To access the "ebook" version, you may log onto www.ibooks.net, click the "About Pets" button and follow the directions.

.Original title: *de Goudvis*
© 2002 Welzo Media Productions bv,
Warffum, the Netherlands
http://www.overdieren.nl
Photos: Rob Doolaard,
Frans Maas, Europet
Drawings: Aquamor (Heja Nederland)
Tanya M. Heming-Vriends
Printed in China

In general

The goldfish is a fish that is not naturally found in the wild. It is generally accepted that the goldfish *(Carassius auratus)* is the domesticated form of the copper-colored crucian or gibel carp *(Carassius auratus gibelio)*.

This carp often displays golden-red color variations that breeders over the centuries have selectively bred and genetically transformed into the goldfish. The copper-colored crucian carp is normally green or brown in color, but of course it was those that displayed this golden-red color that were selected for breeding as goldfish.

Origins

The goldfish is an ancient species. Various documents confirm that breeders in China were already working on this variety in 960 AD. They named the fish "Chin-yij." Scarcely 200 years later, this fish was a popular pet among the nobility. On or around 1173, it was to be found in various varieties in many places. Of course, glass aquariums were not yet available and the fish were often kept in porcelain or earthenware bowls. Outdoors, they could be admired in ornamental ponds.

Around 1500, the goldfish was also to be found as a pet in Japan. Here, this small fish was given the name "Kingyo." The first goldfish arrived in Europe two centuries later. The first examples arrived in England in 1692 when a sea captain brought the fish from Macao (China). Thirty years later the goldfish also arrived in Holland. They were imported from Java (Indonesia) from 1728 onwards. The Dutch quickly realized that there was money to be made from this variety of fish, and there was soon a large number of very efficient breeders

Gold*fish*

in Holland. They played a major role in the spread of these fish throughout Europe. In the years after 1750, the goldfish found many enthusiasts in France. Germany was not far behind, and some thirty years later, there was a busy trade in goldfish there, too. But they weren't cheap pets, and they were used as a status symbol by nobility and wealthy merchants. Prince Griorgi Aleksandrovich Potemkin (1739-1791), a Russian army officer and an important figure during the reign of Catherine the Great, is known to have had various goldfish in the ponds of his winter garden.

Goldfish were introduced in America in 1859. Once these fish became known here, their popularity grew rapidly.

Fish or miniature?
When you think about goldfish, you probably picture in your mind a small gold-colored fish. However, in certain conditions these little fish can grow to nine pounds. The fish we keep in aquariums, of course, can't grow to that size, and ornamental fish in the garden pond don't usually get so big and heavy either.

Appearance
Some fish experts divide the goldfish into two types: the clearly scaled goldfish and the "unscaled" goldfish. The latter also have scales of course, but they are transparent and difficult to distinguish. The body form of the goldfish matches that of an average small carp, but the goldfish doesn't grow as broad. The goldfish is also laterally less flat and clearly rounder.

The scaly varieties initially appear almost colorless or a little silvery. As they grow and mature, they first become black and then red, white, or a mixture of both. The unscaled varieties don't possess the metallic gloss of the scaly type. We sometimes even see subtle colorings of blue or lavender. The young unscaled fish are initially white with black spots and quickly get their final coloring. A splendid unscaled variety is the Shubunkin, which originated in Japan. This fish is blue with red, yellow or red and dark brown, or a combination of these colors.

Feeding in the wild
Although the goldfish is a variety originally bred by man, it is now occasionally found wild in the waters around the Mediterranean Sea. They have also been observed in sub-tropical America. These "wild" goldfish live in both flowing and still waters and eat both animal and vegetable food.

Their animal food consists of fleas, freshwater shrimp, mosquito larvae and worms (including

in general

primarily tubifex) while their vegetable food consists of duckweed, algae and young water plants. Goldfish will also fill their mouths with mud from the bottom, chew on it for a while and finally spit the sand and other residue out. They will have filtered out any pieces of plant or animal remains and eaten them. How they actually do this is not yet precisely known.

A closer look at goldfish: Ichthyology

Ichthyology is the study of fish. The body temperature of a fish is dependent on its environment; they breathe through gills and their skin is covered in bony scales. They also have fins and reproduce by means of eggs without shells. Their body shape is totally adapted to living in water. If you hold a goldfish in your hand it will feel totally slippery because it has no cuticle layer. The smooth mucous layer makes mobility in water easier, and this layer is continuously replenished by glands in the skin. The bony scales (consisting of bony tissue, as the name implies) are formed within the leathery skin and lay on it superimposed like roof tiles.

Movement

The fish's torpedo-shaped body eases movement through water; the transition from head to rump is generally very gradual. Its movement is twisting from side to side, in a wave from head to tail. The pectoral and pelvic fins are used as brakes or for turns and for "standing" in water. The well-developed tail fin (or caudal fin) is actually of secondary importance for movement. All fins consist of bony rays which are connected together by a membrane.

Breathing

Goldfish breathe through the red gills that are easily visible by lifting the gill cover. A gill is built of thin folds of skin which are arranged in a double row along the gill arch. When breathing, the water flows in through the mouth, then through the elaborate gill filaments, along the gills and out again through the gill cover. There are also so-called "lungfish." These fish use their gills in water. When on land, the air bladder takes in swallowed oxygen.

Blood circulation

The heart lays behind the gills and consists of one ventricle and one auricle. A ventral aorta, known as the gill aorta, extends from the ventricle with branches into the gills. The blood fed here is extremely low in oxygen. In the gills, the blood takes in oxygen which is fed into the veins and then circulated into an aorta. This aorta has branches which take oxygen-rich blood to all the body organs which absorb the oxygen and transfer carbon dioxide to the in general

blood. Oxygen-poor and carbon dioxide-rich blood flows through the vessels to the auricle and then again into the ventricle where it is pumped through again. The goldfish thus has a very simple circulatory system.

Digestion

When humans take in food, the digestion process begins in the mouth. This is not the case with fish: the mouth sieves the food out of the water. There are tiny teeth on the gill arches, so-called plankton filters, which stop the food particles. We call that a "gill sieve." The short gullet steers the food towards the stomach, where the digestive process starts. From the stomach, the food enters the intestine where the pancreas and gall-bladder join. Fish have a large liver to form gall.

The intestine and kidneys each have a separate outlet, so fish (except sharks) do not have a cloaca as such.

The swim bladder

The swim bladder lies between the liver and the kidney and is usually connected with the gullet. However this connection doesn't exist in some fish such as bass, sticklebacks and cod. Sharks, rays and flatfish have no swim bladder at all. The swim bladder is full of

Goldfish

gasses that have a totally different pressure and composition to that of normal air. These gasses practically match those gasses that have an external effect on the fish. Using the connection tube with the gullet, or by means of the blood (the swim bladder wall contains a network of fine capillaries) fish can pass gasses to the swim bladder, but also pump gas out of it, for example oxygen, if the blood needs it.

As a fish passes gas to the swim bladder, its specific gravity drops, causing it to rise. If gas flows out or passes into the blood, the opposite happens and the fish sinks. We call this organ a "hydrostatic" organ. Researchers have performed many experiments with fish in this area. For example, they weighed a fish down by attaching tiny weights to it. The result was that the quantity of gas in the air-bladder increased. As the researchers made the fish lighter by tying corks to it, the gas quantity reduced.

Nervous system

The nervous system is formed by the cerebral and spinal marrow and the nerves that branch out from them. Fish have no eyelids and have limited movement for their eyes. They can distinguish between colors. Their highly sensitive scent organs are in two grooves on their head, but are not connected with their mouth. Their sense of taste is in the mouth and very probably in the whiskers that many fish possess. Water movements are sensed by the so-called lateral line that runs along the side of the fish. This is a system consisting of a large channel and a network of many tiny side-channels with sensory cells containing jelly-like protuberances. We find cells with such protuberances on the skin too, which are pressed aside by flowing water and then stimulate the sensory cells.

Hearing

Fish have an elaborate ear, which is usually connected with the swim bladder. There are fish varieties that don't have this connection and they have substantially poorer hearing. There is no cochlea present as there is in the human ear.

Feeding your goldfish

Of course, you need to know how best to feed your fish.

Water layers and feeding

Fish live in certain "layers" of water. This has a major influence on their eating habits. Those that live at the bottom gather their food from the ground. This may be worms or larvae. Fish in the middle layers of the water live on insects such as midges and mosquitoes, on larvae or crustaceans such as water fleas. Surface feeders live on insects that live on the surface or land on it.

How much food?

Some fish can literally eat themselves to death, so never give too much food. There is often enough food in the aquarium itself. These may be eggs laid by one type of fish that are a real treat for others. Cardinal Tetras are known to be egg eaters. Guppies, Black Mollys and other fish like to eat algae.

Although it depends on the fish in your aquarium, there is a rule of thumb you can follow. Feed your fish with pauses of at least two days and make sure you feed only small portions so that nothing falls to the bottom where it might rot.

Types of food

There are three types of food you might use if you want to keep a flourishing aquarium with happy fish. There is live food consisting of tiny living animals such as mosquito larvae and water fleas. You can buy frozen food in the pet store and there is the well-known dry food.

Live food

You can often buy live food in good aquarium shops. There are some aquarium lovers that catch their live food themselves in ditches and ponds. If you decide to do that remember to use a white bucket in which you can see precisely what you've caught and prevent introducing unwanted guests into your aquarium. The following are a few examples of live food. Very popular are water fleas and so-called copepoda. There are also various types of mosquito and midge larvae. Red midge larvae are larvae of the "dancing midge" (*Chironomus plumosus*). You might encounter white midge larvae when catching water fleas. These are the larvae of a midge that doesn't bite and you can recognize it by its transparent body. The white midge larva can be bought in aquarium shops in tubes filled with water and larvae. The larvae can be kept for quite a while in the tube without food or oxygen. Be careful with black midge larvae, which are those of the biting midge. Don't bring too many into your home or you'll wind up with an infestation of midges.

Frozen food

Almost all live foods can also be bought in frozen form. As a beginner, these may be your best choice to avoid introducing irregularities into your aquarium. However, there is one major disadvantage in frozen foods. They don't encourage your fish to hunt, although that is part of their nature.

Dry food

Dry food is available in all shapes and sizes. The disadvantage of dry food is that most drift on the surface. Some fish gobble the food up at the surface and take in so much air that this gets into their intestines and can kill them. You can prevent this by soaking the food before you sprinkle it in your aquarium.

A home for your goldfish

You can keep goldfish in various ways, but one home is not the same as another, and it is important to give your goldfish a proper place to live.

In this section, we discuss the advantages and disadvantages of two forms of home. You will learn what requirements goldfish have in terms of their living environment.

The pros and cons of a fishbowl

The advantages of a fishbowl are of benefit only to the fish-owner. The fish, of course, would benefit from much more space to live in, but most fishbowls aren't large enough.

You can place a fishbowl practically anywhere, but not every place is suitable. In front of a window in the full sun, for example, is a poor place. An advantage of a fishbowl is that you can move it around easily, and it's a simple job to keep it clean. A disadvantage is that there is room for two small fish at most. Most fishbowls hold some one gallon of water and that's really only just enough for one fish.

Water surface

But it's not the size of the bowl and the amount of water it can hold that is most important for your goldfish. They would benefit more from having enough surface area. A goldfish breathes by taking in oxygen from the water, and it also gives off carbon-dioxide into the water. This always happens close to the surface. If the surface area is too small, the water absorbs too little oxygen and can not give off enough carbon-dioxide. Your fish will die. There are fishbowls in the stores

Goldfish

a home for your goldfish

with a very narrow neck. If you fill this to the top with water thinking you're doing your fish a favor, then there's a good chance that your fish won't be able to get enough oxygen. Fill the bowl only halfway with water and the surface is then usually much larger.

Furniture

A fishbowl must be equipped just like an aquarium so that it's comfortable for its resident(s). There is a huge assortment of undergravels, hideaways and plants available. You can chose gravel in many colors, rocks, filters and even plastic plants.

Housekeeping

It's easy to forget to clean a fishbowl, but it is very important. Because of the relatively small dimensions, the water can get dirtier much quicker than in an aquarium. When you clean your fishbowl, you must temporarily put the fish in a bucket or a tank with water. Then you can put in fresh water, clean the sand, gravel and rocks properly and, if you use a filter, you must also clean that. Don't forget to check the filter for any faults. A fishbowl should be cleaned once a week. The fresh water should be at approximately the same temperature as the fish are used to swimming in. Many a goldfish has suddenly gone to the great fishpond in the sky after a sudden dive into cold water. The animal can go into shock.

Pros and cons of an aquarium

Fish will enjoy life in an aquarium far more than in a fishbowl because of the extra space. And with an aquarium, you can create a beautiful natural backdrop in your own home. The only things you need are the aquarium itself, some rocks, sand or gravel, wall covering and plants. You can get years of pleasure from an aquarium. There are various models available in stores, and you can choose glass or polyester containers. A disadvantage of an aquarium is that it is somewhat more expensive, especially compared to a fishbowl, but you may be able to get over that hurdle by looking for a good second-hand aquarium.

A place for an aquarium

From now on, we're talking about an aquarium, but by far the most points we cover in this small book also apply to goldfish kept in a fishbowl.

Before filling an aquarium, you need to think about where it is to stand. Once an aquarium is equipped, it's not easy to move, if only because of the weight. The choice of location will depend largely on the size and shape of your aquarium, and you also need to consider the table or cupboard you're going to put your aquarium on. This needs to be strong enough to carry the weight. If that's not the a home for your goldfish

Calico fantail

case there's a risk that the cupboard, shelf or whatever else your aquarium stands on will sag. Your aquarium is then not getting even support and may crack. The room's floor must also be strong enough to hold the weight. With concrete floors this will not be an issue, but wooden floors might pose a problem.

If you do decide you're strong enough to move a full aquarium remember the following. Because of the weight and pressure of the water, panels may break or crack. On a frame aquarium, the seams or joints may start to leak. Finally, if you slosh the water around too much, your fish may go into shock. There are other points you need to consider when placing your aquarium. There must be electricity sockets nearby for filter and light connections. Hide cables behind the aquarium so that nobody can trip over them. Make sure you can get at the aquarium easily to clean it or to feed your fish. Try not to put it close to a door. The vibrations caused by the opening and closing of a door can be disastrous for your fish, and if you own a cat, you need to keep an eye on that as well.

Light
Your aquarium must never stand in

Goldfish

a home for your goldfish

the full sun, but light is also very important. Algae can form if there's too little light getting into the aquarium, and the plants in the aquarium won't flourish either. If you do want to locate your aquarium close to a window, chose a window facing east. In the winter, you certainly won't have enough sunlight and you'll have to add some light. Most aquariums are fitted with a light hood as standard.

Too much direct sunlight can cause the water temperature to rise, and you need to be careful on this. A temperature higher than 75°F will feel very uncomfortable for your goldfish, mainly because the quantity of oxygen drops quickly in warmer water. This can have fatal consequences in an aquarium with several fish. (Gold)fish can't handle temperature fluctuations well, so never put an aquarium in a drafty location or anywhere close to heaters or air-conditioners.

Aquarium types

Most aquariums are made of glass or plexiglass and are frameless. This means that the seams are "unbreakable." Many all-glass aquariums do have a top edging, but this is for purely decorative purposes. There are also plastic aquariums for sale but these are not advisable. They are often small, break quickly and are very vulnerable to scratches. If you're serious about your hobby, buy a glass aquarium. The shape is also important. A square container with a large surface area is better for your goldfish than a high model with a smaller water surface.

Dimensions

Before you buy an aquarium, you must know exactly what you want to do with it. "Keeping fish" is not enough information. Firstly, make sure you have enough room for the model you want to buy. Secondly, you need to think about the number of (gold)fish you plan to keep. Goldfish like plenty of room. You can use the following rule of thumb: for each two pints of water there is room for one fish one inch in length. If your goldfish is four inches long, it needs one gallon of water. Also think about the life expectancy of a fish, of course. Young goldfish are still small but, of course, they'll grow, so stick to two pints of water for these fish, too. Goldfish are sturdy in form (flat and wide) and the bigger and sturdier the fish, the more oxygen it needs. Also take into account the fact that goldfish will grow "with" their container. If you give goldfish the freedom of a big aquarium, they will grow very fast. So it's good advice to have an aquarium of at least 16 gallons for five goldfish.

Things you need for an aquarium

A good home for goldfish is more than just an aquarium tank. There are other things you need for a water eco-system to function properly.

In this section you can learn what apparatus and other equipment you need to buy to get maximum pleasure from your aquarium.

Cover panel

Your goldfish won't deliberately jump out of your aquarium, but this is not totally unheard of. If goldfish are seriously frightened, or if the water is dirty and poor in oxygen, they can certainly jump four inches out of the water. A fish may also jump out of the water if it's bothered by parasites or other pests that have attached themselves to its gills. So you need to make sure that the aquarium is equipped with a cover panel.

Cover panels not only stop fish jumping out of an aquarium, they also prevent unwanted substances getting into the water, and they also help prevent too much evaporation. You will certainly notice that droplets of condensation gather on the underside of the cover panel. These mostly drop back into the water and can help cool it down. This can be very useful on warm summer days.

In aquariums with cover panels the water thus stays in longer and that's good news. After all, the more water the more oxygen. Furthermore, more water can handle more droppings and other pollutants.

Light hoods

If you want artificial light in your aquarium then a light hood is the

things you need for an aquarium

best choice. You then don't need a cover panel. Light hoods often work on low voltage, which means you'll need a transformer.

Try to maintain a normal day/night rhythm with the lighting, meaning approximately 12 hours of darkness and 12 hours of light. This will keep algae growth under control and plants will flourish—they react positively to light. During the day, plants absorb oxygen, and during the night they give it off. This is an important process for your aquarium. If the lighting is on 20 hours per day then the plants will only absorb oxygen. The time they have to give oxygen off is too short and over time your plants will wane. Not only is the lighting time (number of hours) and the color of your lighting (some plants need green or red lamps) important, but also the wattage. When buying your aquarium, ask what wattage is required for the light hood that goes with it. There are light hoods that you can put light bulbs in, but a small neon tube is better. A light hood with neon tubes gives off a softer and more natural light and is less costly in consumption. They also give off less heat, reducing the chance of condensation.

Heating elements

Goldfish are cold-water fish, and water at a temperature of 65–68°F is excellent for them. There are also goldfish varieties that can stand lower water temperatures if they have to, so a heating element is not really a necessity. However,

Light hood

Goldfish

things you need for an aquarium

winter weather may mean you need one, especially if you have a small aquarium and live in a house with no central heating. In an aquarium with 5–10 gallons, the water temperature can drop from 70°F to 40–50°F within a few hours. Goldfish can go into shock in water that cold, and will often die or become seriously ill. If you have a heating element, set it at 65°F. Then if the water temperature does drop, it won't bother your fish.

If you're not sure what sort of heating element you need for your aquarium, or you want to be sure the element that was supplied with your aquarium is the right one, use the following rule of thumb:

You need 0.6–1.2 watts for two pints of water. If you have an 18-gallon tank, buy a heating element of 25–50 watts. There are also elements available with a built-in thermostat. These elements sense water temperature fluctuations and switch on as soon as it's necessary. However, these elements do have one small disadvantage; they don't show the actual water temperature. You still need to measure the temperature with the help of a thermometer.

Thermometers
If you want to be serious about your hobby, you must check the water temperature daily with one or two thermometers. There are two types of thermometers. One

Goldfish

things you need for an aquarium

works with a red-dyed alcohol mixture. These thermometers are usually fixed in the aquarium with red suction feet. The other type is attached to the outside wall of the tank with a rubber suction pad. There are also digital thermometers in the stores that you can attach to the outside of your aquarium. Take care when placing thermometers in the water. If they are too close to a heat source they may give a false reading, and you don't want fish colliding with the thermometer.

Filters

Various types of filters are available from pet stores. Most are made as follows: a layer of fiberglass, then a layer of active carbon, then another layer of fiberglass and finally a layer of coarse gravel (the latter prevents the filter becoming blocked). Fiberglass stops fine particles, and active carbon purifies the water. It will also eliminate any smells and ensure a practically constant acidity in the water. Most models are nothing more than an extractor, a combination of two tubes of different diameters. By blowing air through the tube that is fitted below the wide pipe, air bubbles rise to the surface drawing the water with them. This causes a suction effect in the filter chamber.

You can choose between the following types of filters. If you're not sure what type you need, ask for information in a specialty aquarium store or from your local aquarium association.

1. The horizontal internal filter (attached inside the aquarium, directly on top of the sand); this type is the easiest to hide among the fittings in the aquarium (for example behind driftwood, a rock or a group of plants, etc.). A disadvantage is poor performance because the water stream is horizontal.
2. The vertical internal filter (this is also laid on the sand and can be "hidden"). Performance is better than that of the horizontal filter.
3. The vertical external filter. This is perhaps the most efficient type for a goldfish aquarium, despite the fact that it takes more space than the other two types. The filter "sits" in a metal frame and is attached to the outside of the aquarium. The water enters via a siphon (which hangs in the water inside the aquarium) and exits via a cellulose or plastic tube. This is a fast form of filtering.

Air pump

The air pump actually has a dual purpose: firstly, it delivers the energy for the filter to do its work and it serves to pump fresh air into the aquarium. The pump produces compressed air that is delivered to the filter siphon. You can regulate the intake level

Thermometer

Filter

Goldfish

things you need for an aquarium

Air

yourself with a valve; if you put a branch into the pipe you can deliver air to a second point with an aerator stone creating excellent water circulation. You can leave the pump working 24 hours per day, but make sure it is placed a little higher than the water level to prevent any overflowing. Of course, the air sucked in by the air pump must be clean. If people smoke in the room, the air is going to be impure.

Fishnet
You can buy all kinds of fishnets, small or large, in your aquarium store. You may need to take fish out of the aquarium, so make sure the net can be maneuvered freely in the water. Use a net which is not too small. If you have a 10 gallon tank, a net of 6–7 inches across is ideal. Remember that goldfish can jump up once they're in the net, so cover the net with your thumb and index finger before lifting it out of the water. Don't forget to put the net in boiling water for 30 seconds or so before use to ensure it is free of any parasites that may have gathered in it when it was last used. Also be sure to let the net cool before you use it!

Aquarium cleaners
You can clean the inside of aquarium glass with a felt scraper or a blade scraper. Only use a blade scraper if algae have really stuck fast on the pane. Be sure to avoid scratching the glass. You can also use magnets to clean the glass. One magnet on the outside and another inside the tank moved vertically up and down will wipe the algae from the glass. By the way, goldfish like to eat algae so you won't need to clean too much.

Cleaning the floor
Fish droppings and dead leaves from the water plants on the floor of the aquarium must be removed from time to time. If not, there's a risk that the water will become contaminated and depleted of oxygen. The best tool is a small glass or plastic siphon. A rubber

Magnets to clean the glass

Goldfish
22

hose can be used for larger aquariums, with a glass or plastic tube at the end with which you can "sweep" the floor. It works like a vacuum cleaner. Once you've applied suction to the tube, the water will start to flow. Let the water into a bucket, and then filter it through a thick cotton cloth before putting the old water back into the aquarium.

Caring for an aquarium

The phrase "an ounce of prevention is better than a pound of cure" certainly applies to your aquarium. If everything in your aquarium is in order, your fish won't get sick and your plants won't die. This means you need good quality heating, ventilation and filter systems.

Make it a habit to take a quick look at the thermometer whenever you're in the proximity of your aquarium, and check the ventilation system daily. It only needs a few moments and can prevent a lot of heartache. Aerator stones can quickly get blocked by algae and salt deposits causing back-pressure on the pump. Eventually the diaphragm will start to leak. Also check the filter once a week. The water and air tubes can get blocked by algae or slimy dirt. This also applies to the fiberglass and carbon. A blockage means poor water and air output, or none at all. Replace the fiberglass and carbon regularly.

Leave a few shreds of the old fiberglass and two teaspoonfuls of the old carbon in the filter. This activates the biological filtering process. If you don't do this, the aquarium water will stay turbid for a few days. If you've hidden your filter under the gravel, very carefully lift it out and then push it back in once in a while. This will prevent the filter becoming blocked. Be sure to clean the gravel once in a while with a small vacuum cleaner. A lot of dirt can get into the gravel, be it old food remnants, droppings, etc. If you don't keep it clean, it will become a breeding ground for bacteria and fungi.

Fish and stress

It is well known that stress can attack a fish's immune system, making it more vulnerable to disease and parasites. Stress among fish can be caused by having too many fish in the tank, dirty water, too much vibration close to the aquarium, or change. Parasites, bacteria, viruses and fungi lie waiting to attack an over-stressed fish. A fish suffering from stress gradually loses the mucous layer on its skin. Without this layer the fish is inevitably exposed to disease. You should do everything you can to ensure your fish don't suffer from stress.

The aquarium water

Opinions differ widely on refreshing aquarium water. Some

Aquarium vacuum cleaner

things you need for an aquarium

aquarium lovers say you should replace one fifth of the water each week, others say a third. The author of this book has another opinion. If you keep your aquarium in perfect condition, you only need to replace the water after five years. This means your equipment must be in perfect working order and that you remove any dead fish or (parts of) plants from the water immediately.

However, you do need to top the water up regularly. Some water will evaporate after all, especially due to the heating and lighting. As long as you don't need to top up half of the aquarium, but just four pints or so for a 10-gallon tank, then you don't need to worry about the water chemistry.

The following is a good rule: If you have a 10-gallon tank, replace two pints of water each week. Add a little more to compensate for evaporation. In this way, no major chemical changes will happen as you refresh the water. Apart from that, you can use normal tap-water, because all the chemical elements needed are in the aquarium already and tap water will not endanger your fish.

Water contamination
One of the main contaminants in aquarium water is excess goldfish

Goldfish

things you need for an aquarium

food. Feeding goldfish properly is a real art, regardless of whether you feed dry food in flakes, in frozen form or live food. The golden rule is: always feed in driblets, whatever type of food you use. Your fish must have eaten it all within five minutes (although fish eating always looks like they are wolfing it down). Goldfish have no table manners, and they'll keep scoffing food down if they get the chance. They will eat as long as it takes for them to become so heavy that they slowly sink to the bottom of the aquarium and wait there until the food is digested. Fish that eat a lot also leave a lot of droppings in the water, making life hard work for your filter, so you need to be sure that your filter is up to the job. As far as feeding times are concerned follow the rule: fully-grown fish once per day, preferably in the morning; young, growing fish twice a day (mornings and late afternoon); older fish (four years and older) once every two days.

Goldfish

Plants in an aquarium

An aquarium with only fish in it is not natural. Water plants and fish together can make an aquarium like a piece of living nature. However, you do need to be careful what sorts of fish and plants you choose and whether they suit each other.

Ammania senegalensis

Why plants are so important
Under the influence of light, plants generate oxygen, and the goldfish in your aquarium badly need that oxygen. So they can't live without plants. Goldfish also like to nibble at plants and to hide amongst them from time to time. Goldfish will hide themselves if it's busy around the aquarium or there's something causing agitation in the tank.

Plastic plants or living plants?
Plants in a newly equipped aquarium often have a tough time for the first six months or so. This is because the water and bed have not been able to build up enough nutrients. If you choose plants that have too little reserves of nutrients, they may even die.

Some people therefore choose plastic plants. There's no bother with dead plants and they always look nice. Your fish can still hide away and they can't eat the plants away. Goldfish are omnivorous and will eat both animal and vegetable food. Young plants and sprouting leaves are sometimes too much of a temptation. They will also nibble at plastic plants, but you don't need to worry about that. They do this looking for algae and micro-organisms which they eat off the plastic leaves.
If you're a little more persevering, use real plants. These grow and multiply and some bloom with beautiful tiny flowers. You can also put some plastic plants among the real ones, of course. Then you're always sure to have a fine green background.

Goldfish

Living plants

Because goldfish simply will not leave living plants alone, it's important to choose plants with a strong rootstock (from the rootstock grow the roots and stems): *Aponogeton* and some *Cryptocoryne* and *Echinodorus* varieties are excellent examples here. Plants such as the *Vallisneria*, most *Sagittaria*, *Hygrophila* and *Myriophyllum* varieties don't have a rootstock and are hardly likely to survive in an aquarium without nutrient reserves.

Bacopa carolineana

> The pH value represents the acidity level of the water, or more precisely: the concentration of oxygen ions. This is measured on a scale from 1 to 14. The acidity level has even more influence on our fish than the water hardness itself. pH stands for pondus hydrogenii, which means the weight of the oxygen, i.e., the weight of all oxygen ions in one liter of water. Water with a pH value of 7.0 is neutral, and this pH level is important for almost all fish.
>
> If the pH value climbs above 7, then the water is alkaline, if it goes under 7 then the water is acidic. pH levels above 9 and under 5 are fatal for water residents. There are liquid indicators available in specialist stores. There are also test papers and tablets, but paper indicators are the least reliable. If your water is too alkaline, you can use inorganic acids that are available in specialist stores to acidify it.
>
> Always handle these acids with great care. If you get them on your skin you can suffer a nasty burn. Feed the acid into the water through the ventilation tube or the outlet from your filter. Check the pH value again after each dosage.
>
> If the pH value goes under 5, you can bring it back to the right level using calcium hydroxide. However, it is a lot simpler and much more natural to soften the water, and at the same time acidify it with fibrous turf. Ask for more information at your aquarium store or your local club. There are plenty of other methods. If the water is too acidic you can dissolve a little bicarbonate in a glass of water and feed it into your aquarium water. If it's too alkaline then you need to acidify it. You can do this with primary sodium phosphate. This also needs to be dissolved first in a glass of water.
>
> Never be too radical, and keep checking the pH. If the water is still not as it should be, then add a further dose every two days until it's at the right level again.

Cabomba furcata

plants in an aquarium

Alternathera reineckii sessilis

Most of the living plants you can buy in an aquarium store are intended for tropical aquariums. However, you need plants that can survive in cold water at the same temperature as your goldfish (65–70°F). Some plants grow better in acid water, or in water with a low pH value. Your goldfish don't like acid water, so these plants are best left out of your aquarium.

As far as plants are concerned, stick to the following rules:
1. Most plants thrive well in very alkaline water with a pH over 8.
2. Plants also do well in slightly acidic water with a pH of 6.8.
3. Water plants develop well in neutral water: pH 7.0.
4. The same applies to soft alkaline water pH 7.2 to 7.6 (tap water).

Plant lighting

If plants don't get light, they die. Natural sunlight is important for healthy growth and oxygen generation. Unfortunately, the sun doesn't shine exactly 12 hours per day and this means you need to supplement it with artificial light. See *A home for your goldfish* for more information on lighting.

Location and underfloor

The floor of your aquarium is the feeding ground for the plants. You can cover the floor with turf from specialty aquarium stores. One inch is often enough. Over that you can lay a 1 1/2-inch thick layer of gravel. This gives the plants a good chance of not being pulled out by avaricious goldfish. If you're worried about that, you can lay a heavy stone approximately over the spot where the roots are. This will give them extra protection.

To give your aquarium more depth (which makes it look larger), put plants that only grow low towards the front and high growers in the rear corners and against the back panel. You can disguise your heating element(s) and ventilation pumps behind the high-growing plants. It may be useful to take a look at an especially attractive aquarium to see how it has been arranged. This can give you a lot of inspiration.

Plants for the aquarium

There are many plants suitable for your aquarium. In this chapter, we'll cover a number of plants that are excellent for goldfish tanks.

Water sprite *(Ceratopteris thalicroides)*
This light green plant also comes as a drifting plant. It forms spurs on its leaves that stick out of the water. As the plant gets bigger it takes on the form of a fern. It multiplies from the roots and by offshoots. It is easy to keep, grows best in normal, slightly acidic (pH 5–6.5) aquarium water at a temperature between 70° and

plants in an aquarium

Cryptocoryne petchii

80°F. Its fragile, finely-distributed leaves have to put up with a lot, but even small parts of a leaf can develop new leaf buds. The "foot" of the plant must stand just a little above the ground. This splendid plant grows fast. Even goldfish seem unable to hinder its growth. The plant is found over a huge area. It appears in Africa, southeast Asia and tropical parts of America. The best soil for this plant is normal turf.

Cryptocoryne
This plant from the tropics belongs to the arum family. To develop well it needs a lot of light and a good soil (see the water sprite). *Cryptocoryne* varieties possess a well-developed root system. This plant, which has spear-shaped leaves about six inches, is best placed in the foreground. It does not like temperatures below 70°F. The *Cryptocoryne becketii* and *Cryptocoryne willisii* (previously known as *nevellii*) varieties were cultivated for trading in Europe. The former variety originally comes from Sri Lanka and is well suited for our goldfish aquariums.

Java fern
(Microsorium pteropus)
The Java fern is a plant with a strong rootstock. Its leaves are long, in light and dark green and stand out beautifully against a dark background. In cold water, its leaves never get longer than about four inches; in tropical aquariums they can grow to some

plants in an aquarium

Hydrocotyle leucocephala

Apenogeton crispus

10 inches. The roots can attach themselves to gravel, rocks or a piece of driftwood. This plant originated in India and southern China and wide regions of Asia to the Philippines. It will grow even in poor light and can withstand acidic or alkaline water. The temperature must be between 70° and 77°F. Put a heavy stone over the part of the ground where the rootstock is, so that the fish can't pull it free. If you use driftwood, you can carefully attach the plant to it with thin fishing line (available in fishing tackle stores). The Java fern's roots will eventually attach themselves firmly into the wood.

Aponogeton varieties

There are some 45 known varieties of Aponogeton. The majority of these well-known and strong growing plants come from the tropical regions of Asia. The strongest varieties are *Aponogeton crispus*, *Aponogeton undulatus*, and *Aponogeton natans*. From Australia comes the *Aponogeton elongatus*. All varieties need a temperature between 70° and 82°F and water hardness of 60–80 mg/l. They are best kept in larger aquariums (10 gallons or more). They go through a rest period between November until approximately January and then lose almost all their leaves. It can be useful to take the bulb-shaped rootstock out of the ground and lay it in the aquarium water, or keep it in a separate tank until it develops new leaves. Then you can set the rootstock back into the ground. The stems of *Aponogeton undulatus* don't have flowers but bloom with complete miniature plants at the end of its ball-shaped spikes. The flowers of *Aponogeton crispus* and *Aponogeton elongatus* are white. All these plants develop excellently in a sand and turf soil.

Sword plants (*Echinodorus***)**
There are some 50 known varieties of the sword plant. Good foreground plants are *Echinodorus tenellus*, *Echinodorus quadricostatus* and *Echinodorus latifolius* because they need a lot of light. Unfortunately, they don't always survive the attention of permanently hungry goldfish. *Echinodorus bleheri*, however, can be used well. Its leaves are 3 to 3 1/2 inches wide and dark green in color. The flower stem stays underwater and generates new plants. Sword plants need a normal soil, water of 60 to 80

Ammania gracillis

Hard and soft water
When we talk of water hardness, we mean the amount of calcium carbonate that is dissolved in one liter of water. Too much calcium carbonate is harmful to fish, so it's important we know how hard the water is. Hardness is measured in milligrams per liter, so a hardness of 100 mg/l means that 100 milligrams of calcium carbonate are dissolved in one liter. More precisely spoken, hardness in water is caused by dissolved calcium and magnesium salts. Soft water is thus water with low dissolved calcium and magnesium salt levels. Total hardness consists of two components:
1. Calcium and magnesium compounds which, together with carbon dioxide, form so-called temporary hardness.
2. All other calcium and magnesium salts, which cause so-called permanent hardness.

Total hardness is the same as temporary hardness (also called carbonate hardness) plus permanent hardness (non-carbonate hardness). This means that the total hardness less the temporary hardness is the same as the permanent hardness.

The ideal every aquarium lover should strive for is a total hardness of 60 mg/l. Most fish can be bred in this and aquarium plants will flourish. A hardness of 0–30 mg/l means that the water is soft. You can buy various products for measuring the hardness of your water in aquarium stores.

There are various methods to soften water. The first is a softener filter for which you need no knowledge of chemistry. A simple way to get soft water is to mix rainwater or distilled water (can only be made with special equipment, ask your aquarium dealer) with hard water. To get the right ratio you need to know that distilled water has a hardness of 0 mg/l, but is somewhat expensive.

plants in an aquarium

Aponogeton crispus

mg/l hardness and a pH value of about 7. The temperature should be approximately 73°F.

Another "easy" plant for a small aquarium is the *Echinodorus parviflorus*. Once it's established it spreads rapidly, so don't plant it too close to other plants. Both plants need lighting that is not too strong.

Vallis **varieties**
Here too, many varieties are known. The best plant for a goldfish aquarium is and will stay the *Vallisneria spiralis* also known as the *Straight vallis*. This plant has somewhat bluish roots and long, thin light green leaves that can grow up to 30 inches long and be a good half inch wide. It has spirally-rolled white flowers which, after unrolling, appear on the surface. Fertilization then takes place by male flowers that stand on short stilts. The buds are located at the foot of the long leaves and are released, rise to the surface and spring open. The root offshoots take care of multiplication. If the offshoots come out of the ground, there is too little light. If they grow deep, there is too much light. The temperature must never drop below 60°F. Origin: Southern Europe.

Myriophyllum
(milfoil or foxtail) varieties
This gender of plant is characterized by its strongly-branched, vertical stems with rings and it has feather-shaped leaves with slits. If it grows above the surface of the water these slits are then substantially shorter. This plant needs lots of light, but you need to watch out for algae growth. It grows best on a sand floor with a little clay or turf. The Parrot Feather milfoil (*Myriophyllum brasiliense*) is

Hygrophila polysprema

Goldfish
34

plants in an aquarium

excellent for a goldfish tank. Its long and slender stem is soft and curly underwater. The male flowers consist of four pink and white crown leaves. The water level must not be less than 16 inches, otherwise the plant grows out of the water. Origin: South America.

The *Myriophyllum elationoides* has feather-shaped leaves in rings of three to five standing leaves. These leaves are dark blue-green and are one-quarter to three-quarters of an inch long. This plant suits an unheated aquarium well but does need a lot of light. Origin: South America, Northern Brazil, Mexico, Tasmania, New Zealand, and the Falkland Islands.

Myriophyllum hippuriodes is also a slender plant with strong stems and suitable for cold- or warm-water aquariums. Its feather-shaped leaves have six to ten tails. Bi-sexual (self-fertilizing) flowers often appear close to the surface; at the top of the stem are a large number of male flowers. They need a lot of light and like a ground with some clay worked in. Origin: North America and Mexico.

The *Myriophyllum scabratum*, on the other hand, is a fine plant with a large number of forked stems. This plant grows low. Its leaves stand in rings of three, but also opposite each other or in spirals; there are often multiple rings. The plant is soft green in color and stands some 1 1/2 inches high. It does well in cold- or warm-water aquariums and is easy to make cuttings of. The *Myriophyllum scrabratum* is actually indispensable in a breeding tank because fish like to lay their eggs on it. Origin: The eastern part of North America, Eastern Mexico, and Cuba.

Hygrophila **varieties**
The *Hygrophila polysperma* or *Indian Water Friend* is a plant with stems up to 20 inches long. The leaves stand opposite each other, are light green in color and long and oval. They are some 1 1/2 inches long and a half-inch wide. They can withstand temperatures up to 85°F. They need no special lighting but do much better in strong light. Each piece of stem offers the chance of offshoots at the surface. Origin: India.

Cabomba aquatica

Ammania senegalensis

Setting up an aquarium

It sounds really simple: fill aquarium, put in fish and done! Unfortunately it's usually not that simple in practice. There's a lot of work to be done to develop a water ecosystem that is just right. In this chapter you can read how to set up an aquarium properly.

Checking the tank
Before filling the aquarium, you need to check it for leaks. Stand it on a strong horizontal surface and fill it with water. If possible, do this outdoors as long as it's not freezing. Small leaks can be repaired with silicone sealant. If there are major leaks you need to take it back to the aquarium store. Most aquariums are insured by the manufacturer. Inform yourself well before you buy an aquarium or any other equipment for it. Your aquarium must be totally leak-proof before you set it in its final location.

Gravel
Gravel on the bottom of the tank can be very decorative. Make sure it's gravel of good quality. Porous gravel is not recommended because food remnants can get stuck in any openings and contaminate the water. There are all kinds of gravel for aquariums in specialty stores, even in different colors. If you want your aquarium to appear natural, don't buy colored gravel. Before putting the gravel in your tank, wash it thoroughly in a strong stream of water.

Nutrient soil
You may want to leave the central part of your aquarium free of plants and then a floor of properly-washed sharp sand or gravel is sufficient. Gravel alone, however, is not enough in places where you plan plants. There you need to create a good soil (nutrient soil) for your plants. A nutrient soil of turf and coarse sand is sufficient. Some plants need a heavier soil, but you may

Gold*fish*

setting up an aquarium

consider placing these plants on the ground in pots filled with soil suitable for them.

You can buy many nutrient soils ready-made in aquarium stores, but you can also make them up yourself using well-watered turf. Make sure this turf has not been chemically treated. Mix the turf with unwashed river sand (also available in specialty stores). Then put in the soil so that it creates an optical perspective. At the front of the tank it is approximately one inch deep and, at the back, two to three inches. Decorate your aquarium with stones, driftwood and other items. It's advisable not to use more than two different types of stone. Fossilized wood must first be soaked in a bucket of water so that it doesn't float to the surface. You can then nail it to a small plank so that the fish can't knock it over later. Of course you can also make this plank of fossilized wood and cover it with the nutrient soil so that it can't be seen.

You can also build some terraces, but remember that daylight will always shine in obliquely towards the back. Symmetrical terraces often don't look attractive but, of course, it's all a question of taste.

Cover the whole floor with a one inch layer of well-washed sharp sand or gravel. If you're using a ground filter this must naturally lie under the nutrient soil.

First fill the tank with a layer of washed sharp sand or gravel. Then add a nutrient soil for the plants. Secure the nutrient soil with another layer of washed sharp sand or gravel.

Decorate your fish tank with rocks, fossilized wood and create some terraces.

Goldfish

setting up an aquarium

Filling of the aquarium
with water

Fitting the filter
equipment

Rocks
Rocks are not necessary, of course, but they can be ideal decoration for your aquarium. Pieces of rock just laid here and there have no particular function. A better choice is to arrange them in rows above each other (ledges) along the length of the aquarium. If you create some height differences too, this looks particularly attractive. On the terraces you've created you can now put a nutrient soil and washed sand so that plants can grow here too. Then cover the sand with a 1 1/2-inch layer of gravel, otherwise your goldfish will find a way to uproot and nibble the plants to death.

Filling your aquarium
Once your aquarium is in the right spot and is fully equipped except for plants and fish, you can now fill the tank with water. Use cold tap-water; it does not need to be heated and should run for a few minutes before letting it into the aquarium, especially if you live in a house with copper pipes. Copper salts are highly poisonous for fish.

On the illustration (top left) you can see how to run the water into the aquarium. You can also use a hose pipe attached to the tap. Run the water in slowly over a board or stiff grease-free paper to prevent the floor covering being whipped up. You can also lay a plastic garbage bag on the floor

setting up an aquarium

and take it out once the water is still. Only start planting once the tank is three-quarters filled with water. With the water at this level, you can easily work and you can quickly see how the arrangement will look when the aquarium is totally full. Always plant from front to back.

Fitting the heating element and thermostat

You might want to fit the heating and thermostat before you start planting. The advantage is that the water temperature will be more pleasant to work in while you're planting. Furthermore, any excess chlorine will disappear and that is important. Make sure that the heating element and thermostat are at least one quarter underwater.

Before you start planting, leave the water to stand for several hours. Then it will be nice and clear. Switch the heating off before you start planting and check that the temperature is around 68°F.

Planting

If your tank is very deep, use planting sticks when planting. These are also helpful for areas that are difficult to reach (such as those rock ledges). Planting sticks are very useful, particularly because you don't need to disturb the plants that have already been placed. When using a planting stick, you drive the roots into the sand after winding them around the teeth of the planting stick. A disadvantage of planting sticks is that you run a higher risk of damaging the plant's roots. If you want to plant by hand, proceed as follows:

Hold the roots and the foot of the plant between your outstretched thumb and first two fingers. Turn the longer roots round your index finger. Now press straight into the sand until deep into the nutrient soil. The fingers make the hole while the roots are protected. Now stretch your thumb and press the roots into the sand with your index finger. Your thumb and middle finger hold the green part of the plant. Then check the position of the plant. If it's properly lined up then close the hole with your hand. Make sure the foot of the plant is above the gravel, otherwise it will rot away.

After planting

When all the plants have been placed, you can now fill the tank with water. Make sure the water surface is no longer visible from outside. If you have not yet fitted the thermometer, you should do that now. Then close the aquarium with the light hood or cover panel. Make sure the ventilator, filter, thermostat and heating element are all working properly and check the temperature now and again. Once the tank has reached the right temperature, leave the water to stand for two or three

Use a good quality thermometer.

Heating element

Gold**fish**

setting up an aquarium

days. Sometimes it takes a few days before the water has reached an even temperature, but that is not a problem at all. This gives the plants a good chance to establish themselves before the fish arrive, and the water has the chance to become clear again.

Populating your aquarium

Once the temperature is right, wait another week before you let the fish loose in the tank to prevent your fish going into a stress situation with all its possible disastrous consequences. A freshly-equipped aquarium contains a lot of undesirable bacteria that want to establish themselves there. You can avoid this by introducing "good" bacteria, which will quickly take the upper hand, especially if they're supported by a properly functioning filter.

Buying goldfish

The best place to buy goldfish is a good pet store. Don't go in on impulse. Visit the store several times to make sure that it is always well looked after. You can also see whether the personnel pay proper attention to the aquariums. Check that there are not always dead or half-eaten fish drifting in the tanks. An aquarium club in your area can of course give you information about good stores to buy goldfish. Once you've picked the store, you now need to pick the fish. Never buy fish that:
- are sick or damaged
- are constantly snapping for air at the surface
- swim around the floor of the aquarium in a slanted position
- have damaged fins
- display fungal growth around

Goldfish

setting up an aquarium

the mouth
- do not have a streamlined body form, but a hollow, ball-shaped body or one full of "bulges"
- are constantly being chased by other fish

It is very easy to have the "wrong" fish imposed on you, after all you're just a beginner. Always ask for clear answers in the store, or take someone with you that "knows the ropes."

Some important tips
Never put fish into a newly set-up aquarium, because it is not yet biologically in balance. All those ammonia-destroying bacteria are not yet ready for battle. The water temperature is not yet at the right level; the tap-water still contains various chemicals, such as chloride and fluoride, which can be dangerous for our fish. Incidentally, you can quickly clear your aquarium of chloride by dissolving a few drops of chlorine in it. Your fish are highly stressed by having been caught and transported and it certainly won't help them to be set free in an aquarium that is not yet ready to receive its residents. So, once you have prepared your aquarium and filled it with water, let it stand for at least a week before you put fish in.

The first week
- Check that the filter is working properly. A filter working properly produces a strong stream of water and the outflow for the filter should be as close as possible to the surface.
- After you've got the filter working, switch on the heating. Set it to switch on and off at about 65°F. This doesn't always work the first time. Follow the instructions that came with it exactly.
- Put the aquarium lighting on in the morning, and switch it off again before you go to bed.
- After the filter has been cleaning the water for about 24 hours, then the chloride has very probably vanished. Now you need to put the "good" bacteria into the aquarium. To do this, buy a handful of used gravel at the pet store. There will be more than enough "good" bacteria in this to populate your aquarium effectively. At the same time as the gravel, buy a healthy baby goldfish, which you put into the aquarium together with the bacteria. The baby fish will produce enough ammonia to feed the good bacteria; in turn, these quickly form colonies.
- Don't be disappointed if you notice that your aquarium has become a little cloudy after a few days. This happens because the unwanted bacteria are trying to establish themselves in your aquarium. This is finally stopped by the introduction of the "good" bacteria. The filter must be working continuously. Only put your goldfish in when the aquarium is totally clear.

The Common Goldfish

The goldfish and its varieties

Many varieties of goldfish have been bred over the course of time. People began to breed various shapes and colors, especially in China and Japan. They make use of sudden mutations and selectively cultivate these.

In this chapter, you can read about the various varieties of goldfish to help you make the right choices for your own aquarium. To cultivate different varieties, breeders select fish with deviating forms into breeding tanks. The breeders use well-proven methods to establish such new varieties and preserve them for posterity. Sudden changes in shape and color (mutations) are common among goldfish. A doubling of the caudal or anal fin, loss of the dorsal fin or the appearance of protruding eyes are regular occurrences. If left alone, these mutations will revert to the goldfish in its original color and shape after a few generations.

The Common Goldfish
In the previous chapters, we often spoke of "the goldfish." This "common" goldfish is a pretty fish with a bright orange coloring and a metallic gloss. Its head should be wide in form. If you look at the head from front to rear, it should gradually flow into the body via the dorsal and pelvic fin to the base of the tail fin. The base of the tail should be about the same width as the snout measured just in front of the eyes. The dorsal fin should start at the highest part of the back and end at the base of the tail.

The common goldfish can thrive not only in an aquarium, but can also be kept in a pond. It can stand cold water better than most of the other varieties. A goldfish kept in a 10-gallon aquarium and

the goldfish and its varieties

properly cared for will eventually grow to a length of eight inches. Bigger aquariums give the fish more opportunity to grow and goldfish of about eight inches are no exception here. In large (park) ponds, the common goldfish can easily grow to 12 inches.

The Comet Fish

This is a tough little fish, regardless of whether its kept in an aquarium or a pond. This variety is a fast swimmer and is very similar in appearance to the common goldfish. However, its tail is noticeably longer. This applies especially to its forked caudal fin, which is often as long, or even longer, than the body. It is normally a brilliant deep red in color and possesses an orange metallic gloss. In some cases these fish have mother-of-pearl colored scales. The comet doesn't grow as fast as the common goldfish and will not get as big. In a large aquarium or a spacious pond it will grow to a maximum of some 7 inches, although over time there have been exceptions with fish up to 10 inches long. The gradual elongation of the caudal fin begins when the fish is only two inches long.

The Shubunkin

This fish originally came from Japan and dates back to the beginning of the last century. In China, this fish is known as "Chuwen-chin." The variegated Shubunkin has bright patterns of color and is often named "calico" because of that. It has mother-of-pearl-colored scales, which make

The Comet Fish

Goldfish

45

the goldfish and its varieties

The Fantail

brown, yellow, red, peach, gray, orange, white and black colors possible. Shubunkins with blue colorings are the most valuable.

There are two forms: the London Shubunkin and the Bristol Shubunkin. The London form, in terms of color, is very similar to the common goldfish. It is somewhat smaller and seldom grows beyond six inches or so. In shape and size, the Bristol Shubunkin is similar to the London variety, but its tail has grown to a very wide, forked fin. This fin is not as long as the Comet's however.

Both varieties are very sought after among fish lovers, although the Bristol wins in the popularity stakes against the London. Both these varieties, along with the others covered above, are very suitable for beginners. They are excellent swimmers and can stand an inadvertent knock or two.

The Fantail
The Fantail is one of the oldest varieties of goldfish. Its metallic orange color should be deep and bright. The fish is shaped like an egg with a long and flowing tail. It is the most common fancy breed available to the average fish owner.

The Ryukin
The Ryukin is the Japanese version of the Fantail. This variety's back is curved very high.

The Ryukin has twin caudal fins that can become as long as six inches and it otherwise has a "wide" look. This fish is found in red, orange, black and white, with two-colored and sometimes three-color markings.

These goldfish have a short, more or less egg-shaped and certainly not flat body. Looking at the head from above and from one side to the other, it is solidly built and very wide. It's difficult to tell precisely where the head ends and the body begins. Some varieties have a dorsal fin, others not. Good fish have a high, stiff dorsal fin, which is normally spherical along the top edge. So it's not

Goldfish

"hollow" as in the case of "flat" bodied goldfish. The back of those fish without a dorsal fin should be smooth, without "lumps" and indentations.

The Japanese Goldfish or Wakin

Experts believe that this goldfish was originally bred in Japan where it became known as the Wakin. This variety is characterized by the fact that it has twin tails and an oval body. Apart from this "twin" tail it is very similar to the common goldfish in appearance. The overall impression is of a fantail, with the exception that all its fins appear very delicate. The long dorsal fin is carried vertically and has a rounded outer edge. There remains some space between the caudal and dorsal fins. This exceptionally graceful fish can grow to seven inches in length, of which four inches is the tail. The variety is found with three different types of scale, so it goes without saying that in can be in a wide variety of colors. The Wakin is one of the most elegant goldfish but, sadly, also one of the most sensitive. This is because of the shape of its swim bladder, which reacts badly to very cold water. The fine tail and body fins are also easily damaged because of their structure; rocks and items with sharp edges do not belong in their aquarium. This goldfish is not very suitable for the beginner.

The Shubunkin

the goldfish and its varieties

The Moor

The Telescope fish (Demekin)

This remarkable variety has large eyes that look almost as if they've been mounted on an ice-cream cone. The eyes of an adult fish often stand one-tenth of an inch from the head. One assumes that this fish originated in China and was bred there in the 19th century. In China this fish is called "dragon-eye" or "dragon fish." Japan was also very interested in this variety, and at the beginning of the 20th century, there were many breeders of the telescope in Japan, where it is known as the Demekin. Apart from its strange eye structure this fish is almost identical to the fantail. It is never bigger than approximately eight inches. It is indeed ironic that this fish, with all that eye equipment, has very poor eyesight. For this reason, you can't keep it with a lot of other fish because it has trouble finding its food. In a tank full of goldfish, the other types will snap the food away before the telescope fish's very eyes. The telescope fish must be kept together with its own kind or with other similarly handicapped fish.

Goldfish

the goldfish and its varieties

The Celestial
This fascinating variety thanks its eyes for its name. These are pointed upwards towards the sky. This fish was bred by the Chinese who gave it the name "Ch'aot'ienyen." This means "the dragon that looks to the sky." The English name is "Celestial," which means "seen in the sky." There are certain advantages with this eye position: all the insects and other treats such as plant particles that swim by above are quickly detected and consumed. The eye structure is immobile; they can not look down or turn from right to left.

You'll get more pleasure from these fish if you keep five celestials together, without other fish. Most of these fish have no dorsal fin and are pinkish in color, but metallic-colored and variegated varieties have also been bred. There is even a very strange black form, which is known in Japan under the name of "Demeranchu." Celestials are fish for the advanced enthusiast. They are also very expensive.

The Moor
This variety is very similar in appearance to the telescope fish, except that it is velvety black in color and its eyes do not stand out so far from its head. The telescope eyes are in the normal "goldfish position," although there are fish whose eyes stand pointed straight ahead or downwards. This fish is quite sturdy and, perhaps for this reason, is often kept in garden ponds.

Many goldfish beginners are interested in the Moor, perhaps because the black color is "in." However, the Moor's eyes are also very vulnerable, so its aquarium must be clear of any sharp rocks or edges. As the Moor gets older, its deep black color very gradually attains a bonze-like tint.

The Water Bubble-Eye
The Water Bubble-Eye is very well known. There are large fluid-filled sacs that grow underneath each eye. The variety is still bred at full speed in the Chinese province of Kwangtung where it is much in demand, but it remains a bizarre fish with large "ramparts" under the eyes. Furthermore, it has no dorsal fin. One part of the eye (the "balloon") is filled with a gelatinous fluid. The actual eye itself is pointed upwards, although not as markedly as that of the telescope fish. The balloon is actually the swollen bottom eye-lid. These balloons start to develop when the fish is some six to nine months old, and by the time the fish is two years or so older, these balloons can be very big. It is then practically impossible for the fish to swim properly.

Goldfish

the goldfish and its varieties

The Water Bubble-Eye

It will be obvious that an aquarium with bubble eyes must not contain any rocks with points or sharp edges, because the balloons can very easily burst, and they will only grow back very slowly, if at all. This makes the fish extremely vulnerable to infections. We recommend you to only keep these fish in your aquarium when you've become a little more expert in your hobby. Furthermore, you should not combine these fish with other fish species or goldfish varieties, but only with other bubble eyes. That does not need to be boring, because the bubble eye has been bred in many

The Oranda

Goldfish

different colors, both in metallic and mother-of-pearl.

The Oranda

This splendid, stately swimmer, though somewhat strange in appearance, is highly popular. It originated in Japan where it is always called by its full name, Oranda shishigashiri, and suits the advanced fish-lover. The Oranda was first bred in 1840 and is very similar to the fantail. The major difference is the protuberance that is generally found on its head, and is also called the "hood." The hood must not cover the whole face and should be along the side of the head at most. These fleshy growths look like small bunches of grapes and start to develop when the fish is 2 to 2 1/2 years old. Touching the hood, it feels very soft, but is actually stronger than you might expect and damage is rare. The fish has good eyesight and can easily avoid obstacles. But the hood does have some disadvantages. Bacteria, fungi and dirt can easily settle in the folds, with a risk of infection. Clean water at just the right temperature is extremely important.

The Oranda is often found in metallic gloss, with base colors from copper-red to bright red. The cherry-red varieties are a real pleasure to behold. It is interesting that these splendid and particularly clear colors are already present at a very young age. There is always a cherry-red "area" on the top and the sides of the head. This area will gradually be covered by the hood. This fish is very delicate and is also now found in a brown color (chocolate Oranda) and in blue-white. All together, this is a fish for advanced enthusiasts. Moreover, the Oranda is definitely not cheap. It is sometimes kept as a pond fish, but because of its delicate nature needs to be brought indoors in fall and winter and put in a spacious, well-equipped aquarium.

The Lionhead

The Lionhead is the Chinese version of the Japanese Ranchu variety. Outside Japan too, this fish, which has no dorsal fin, has been able to gain a very positive reputation. It is often kept together with other slow-swimming goldfish.

The Lionhead is fully grown in about two years, and at that time it is about 5 inches long. It has short fins, including twin caudal and anal fins. Apart from its mouth, nostrils and eyes, the whole head is covered by a fleshy growth, reminiscent of a small bunch of grapes. This is what this fish thanks for its name: there are people who see a lion's mane in this growth. This fish is not suitable for beginners, it is far too sensitive.

The Oranda

The Lionhead

Breeding goldfish

Once you've got some experience in keeping goldfish, you can move on to the next stage in your hobby: breeding goldfish. This chapter looks at the reproductive biology of the goldfish.

It would be going too far to look at the breeding of the different varieties and mutations. The points in this chapter that apply to aquarium goldfish also apply broadly to pond fish.

Gender differences

It is almost impossible to tell the gender of young goldfish. Outside the breeding season, it is very difficult or practically impossible to tell the difference with even fully-grown fish. The best method is to buy approximately six young goldfish which you keep as breeding fish; the chance is pretty good that you'll have at least one is of a different sex. When fish are fully grown, you can only tell the difference between the sexes during the spring. The females swim around with fat bellies full of eggs. On goldfish with egg-shaped bodies, the easiest way to see this is by looking at the fish from above and comparing its "streamline" with other fish of the same variety. The males are more slender. Watch out for white "pimples" on the head and gills during early spring, just before the breeding season. Fish that have these pimples are without doubt males. After the males have fertilized the eggs (roe) with their milt, these pimples disappear. During the breeding period both genders are more intensive in color, but especially the male.

Preparation

You can get the breeding process going yourself by keeping the breeding tank water at 52°F for a few weeks and then slowly warming it up again. As the water temperature increases you also give more food than normal. This food should also be rich in proteins, and there are various brands available in specialty stores. Live food, such as tiny worms and shrimp also need to be on the menu. If you can't provide these yourself, you can buy them in an aquarium supply store. It is also important that the breeding tank is tightly planted with *Myriophyllum* (water milfoil), because goldfish particularly like to lay their eggs on this variety's leaves.

Mating behavior and spawning

Goldfish are not monogamous. This means they have no particular partner. Furthermore, a male goldfish will try to fertilize as many females as possible. The mating behavior of the male is fascinating to watch. He will follow the various females around for several days. During this first phase, both sexes become brighter in color. Then the male will pick a female that he tries to steer into the thickest vegetation. After several hours of intense chase (also called "driving") the female will place herself between the plants to spawn. The male presses the female against the plants and both move in a circular or spiral pattern. During these movements the eggs are "released" and the male's milt (sperm cells) is also injected into the water, directly beside the eggs. As the eggs now swirl in the water, they attach themselves to the plants with the help of sticky threads. The milt falls onto the eggs, penetrates

Goldfish

breeding

them, and fertilization is complete. After a few minutes, the male and the female separate, but it won't take long for the male to start driving again.

After two or three hours the spawning process is complete. An adult female goldfish with a well-formed body can lay some 10,000 eggs per season. Once spawning is complete, the male and the female should be removed from the breeding tank. If you don't do this they will both start enthusiastically eating the freshly-laid eggs.

Development of the young

Goldfish eggs look like transparent beads for the first 58 hours. The incubation period is five to seven days depending on the water temperature (70°F). At a temperature of 65°F it lasts seven to eight days. Not all the eggs will develop into young goldfish; some eggs will become overgrown with fungus and look like little

breeding

balls of cotton wool. It's best to remove these from the aquarium and then mix a few drops of methylene-blue into the water.

After three or four days you can already perceive the eyes and the heart-beat in the egg; the baby fish also wriggles constantly and wants to escape from the egg. The yolk, with the fish attached to it is clearly pigmented by the fifth day, and between the fifth and seventh day the fish will find its way out of the egg. The tail emerges first. We still call fish at this stage "larvae." This larvae, along with the hundreds of its brothers and sisters, will attach itself to the aquarium plants, and to the glass in the corners of the tank. After several hours (this can even take a day) they let go and start to really swim. They hungrily look for food. At the tenth day the yolk is almost gone and the all the young fish's food reserves have vanished.

Bringing up the young

As soon as the young "fry"(as the young goldfish are now called) start searching for food, the most critical period in their lives begins. If there's not enough food they will quickly die. You, as breeder, will lose the most fish during this period, so make sure you feed the young well and often. You can buy special goldfish breeding food (in powder form) from specialty stores. "Live" food, such as baby shrimp and microscopic worms, must not be forgotten. This is also available in specialty stores. It is often sold deep-frozen, you must definitely let it thaw completely before using it.

Goldfish larvae are almost colorless in the beginning, but they become whitish after a few weeks. At two months they are a pale yellow. Then the fish gradually turn into their true color. When a fish is fully grown it finally displays its final, "permanent" color.

Fish ailments

One of the worst things that can happen to an aquarium is the outbreak of a disease. A goldfish that doesn't behave normally, looks an odd color or whose fins and tail are not spread wide may be sick. Many goldfish suffer a long time because their owner didn't realize that his fish were sick.

This chapter will cover some diseases that you might encounter when keeping goldfish. We have also tried to present as many treatments as possible.

Medications

Lesson number one in preventing disease in your aquarium is that you should not start putting in medications too quickly. Aquarium stores have a whole world of medications for sale that can help you get rid of a disease. But there are huge numbers of fish that have died because too drastic action was taken, and medications weren't administered properly. If you use medications, read the instructions carefully beforehand. Before you start giving your fish medications, you would do well to ask an experienced aquarium enthusiast (ask at your local aquarium club), or ask the specialist at your aquarium store. Medication is not the only response in many cases. Experienced fish-lovers can probably give you a lot of advice. You would be wise to follow it.

Swim bladder paralysis

A fish can suffer from paralysis of the swim bladder. It can no longer swim and will slowly sink to the bottom of the aquarium. The animal is extremely apathetic and if it does swim, then it will be in spurts on its side or upside down. There's not a lot you can do about swim bladder paralysis, although increasing the water temperature in the early stage can sometimes deliver positive results. Sometimes swim bladder paralysis

fish ailments

results from constipation, so a diet change may help. Consult your local aquarium store for advice.

White spot or "Ich"
White spot is probably among the best known fish diseases. White spot is a parasite that is present in many aquariums, the *Ichthyophthirius multifilis*. A healthy fish can offer it resistance, but if there's one fish in your aquarium with weakened resistance, the parasite will settle on it. Once that's happened, the parasite multiplies immediately. These offspring can then "attack" healthy fish too and cause an explosive development of the disease.

If your fish has this disease, you will see irregular white spots over its whole body, the tail and other fins. You must act fast to prevent an explosion of the disease. There are many commercial ich remedies on the market. If you suspect this disease, seek advice from your local aquarium store.

The Freshwater Louse (*Argulus foliaceus*)
This is a highly-contagious parasite measuring about one-fifth of an inch wide which clamp onto the fish and do not let go. The lice suck blood from the fish through the scales and skin, and the area of the bite may also become infected. Affected fish should be separated from the others, and a commercial treatment available at your pet store can be used in both tanks.

White spot or "Ich"

Some symptoms of fish ailments.
Above: swollen abdominals, open scales, and hanging fins.

"Eaten" fins

Goldfish

fish ailments

Anchor worm
This is another contagious parasite which, unlike the louse, burrows under the scales creating a red, raised area. Seek professional care if this parasite is suspected.

Tumors
Goldfish can suffer from a variety of tumors which appear as small lumps or bumps. A veterinarian can remove these surgically.

Velvet
This is a highly-contagious fungal disease which starts as a fuzzy area and spreads to cover the skin with a dull, velvety coating. Again, pet stores have commercial treatments for this.

Fungal infections
Fungal infections can occur whenever a fish is injured for whatever reason. Fungi normally present in the water attack the injured tissue. White fuzzy fungal growth appears around the area. Commercial treatments are available.

White fuzzy fungal growth

Disinfection
Following treatment of any contagious disease, all parts of the aquarium must be thoroughly cleaned.

Goldfish

facts on the web

Sources of Information on the Internet

The Goldfish Society of America
www.goldfishsociety.org
Devoted to the successful keeping and enjoyment of goldfish.

The Goldfish Sanctuary
www.petlibrary.com/goldfish/goldfish.html
Dedicated to the humane treatment of fish everywhere.

Goldfish Information and Ideas
www.geocities.com/Tokyo/4468/
A site that has useful information about goldfish care and links to breeders and goldfish products.

goldfishconnection.com
www.goldfishconnection.com
Dedicated to the serious hobbyist. It offers for sale various goldfish breeds and products.

facts on the web

Goldfish

profiles

Profiles of goldfish

The Common Goldfish

The Fantail

The Moor

The Shubunkin

The Comet Fish

The Oranda

The Oranda

The Water Bubble-Eye

The Lionhead

The Calico Fantail